Your Ticket to Explore

Essential Preparation For Your
Translator Marketing Adventures

Sarah Silva

Business Translated Publishing

Copyright © 2023 by Sarah Silva

All rights reserved.

No portion of this book may be reproduced in any form without written permission from the publisher or author, except as permitted by U.K. copyright law.

Contents

Ready For Take Off?   1

1. You Deserve First Class   7
2. Why Motivation Is A Poor Travel Companion   19
3. The Dastardly Detours Of Your Brain   29
4. Marketing – The Mountainous Megabeast Rears Its Head…   41
5. The Great Unknown   49
6. Refining Your Route   59
7. The Journey To Yes Is Paved With Good Objections   67
8. Curious Explorers In Action   75
9. Excited To Explore   83

The Explorer's Manifesto   89

References and Recommended Resources   91

About the Author   92

Acknowledgements   93

Ready For Take Off?

To the average eye, it was a boring beige bundle of fabric and straps. To me, my new backpack was a thing of beauty. I propped it up against my wardrobe, visualising it filled with specially selected clothes and my all-seasons sleeping bag. That rugged piece of kit – 65L capacity with a zip-off daypack no less – was going to be my portable home with everything I needed for my Big Travel Trip around the globe. It promised independence and flexibility, travel and adventure, and confidently assured me it would stick by me in all weathers, terrains and whatever challenges lay ahead. And it represented the culmination of months of research.

The destination kept changing. First, I was going solo and planned to teach English in Togo. Then my friend Julia mentioned she fancied travelling too, so teaching got scrapped in favour of seeing more of the world. For hours on end we debated routes and how long we could stretch our time away. To finance the trip, I worked in a paper mill doing tests on pulp and helping with chemical trials. At night, I planned my trip, researching costs and figuring out if I'd need visas or vaccinations.

Finally, the big day came. I'd done my research. But was it enough?

Yes and no. You can prepare as much as you like but research only gets you so far.

If you've never experienced a particular culture or climate you can only base your preparation on other people's perspectives and an educated guess. The problem is, that doesn't give you the full picture and is nowhere near the immersive experience you get when your boots hit the ground in a new environment. When planning my travels, I had no idea I would be actively seeking out wild leopards without a guide in South Africa, cycling around central Tokyo while jetlagged, or driving a questionable car along railway tracks near Mordor. But that's what happened. That was my experience.

Fast forward to a few years later in my translation business. After working with agencies and getting established, I grew restless. I wanted to grow my income and my free time. So I set about making changes in the same way I approached that Big Travel Trip. Lots of research, learning from others, and taking a few tentative steps in different directions, all in an attempt to gain higher-paying direct clients. But it was only when I started taking action and having conversations with potential clients that I got the *experience* I needed to move my translation business forward.

If you're a planner like me, you might enjoy the anticipation and build-up and need time to bring your exciting ideas to life, whether that's due to budget or other restrictions or a lack of knowledge about what lies ahead. Perhaps you can see the destination but aren't sure how to pick a route or what stops you might need or want to make along the way. Maybe you've stopped and started several times because something didn't feel right, you weren't quite ready, or maybe you still don't feel adequately prepared for the next stage of your business.

This is why I've written this book. First, to help you explore any obstacles that are getting in your way and second, to transform your concerns and fears about marketing into excitement about the voyage of discovery. You'll feel inspired to head off on mini business adventures that you can look back on with a sense of accomplishment, knowing that you now have what you need to move *your* business forward. In a few hours, you'll have earned your ticket to explore.

My wish for you

My aim with this book is to offer a new perspective on marketing. I won't be shoving you off a cliff into the icy ocean depths beneath – there are plenty of books and resources available already that tell you to 10x your income by diving headfirst into pushy sales tactics that no one likes or needs. This slim volume is part of my quest to tame the mountainous marketing beast into a pocket-sized pet you can take with you on your travels. Travels to destinations such as 'new clients' and 'extra income in your pocket'. And wouldn't it be nice to enjoy the ride and delight in the scenery along the way?

Sit back with your choice of beverage and consider the possibilities as I take you on a journey of exploration from the comfort of your favourite reading spot. I've even thrown in a few tales from my own travels to entertain you along the way. Are you ready?

Starting point

Travel broadens the horizons, so take a snapshot of where you are now because we're about to go exploring! You'll find suggested actions at the end of each chapter which will help take you from anxious traveller to curious explorer in business and marketing. I've combined all the actions in a handy *Ticket to Explore Action Log* that you can download from BusinessTranslated.com/TicketToExplore and use to document your journey. I do love a good travel diary!

Let's start by opening up your action log or a fresh page in your notebook and answering the following two questions:

1. On a scale of one to ten, how do you feel about marketing your business?
   1 = I'll do everything I can to avoid it including, but not limited to, cleaning the toilet.
   10 = Lemme at it, I just need pointing in the right direction and I'm raring to go!

2. What's your biggest marketing challenge right now?

If you'd like to share, I'd love to hear from you. Send your answers to Sarah@BusinessTranslated.com and use the subject line: My Ticket To Explore – starting point

* * *

Now we're ready for our first stop. Fasten your seat belt because we're going to start by addressing the main barrier to you upgrading to first-class clients.

Chapter 1

You Deserve First Class

Have you ever heard the adage 'It's who you know that counts'? On a trip to Vancouver, I took that advice to heart and asked my husband's aunt – who worked for an airline – if she could do some magic and get us a free upgrade. My friend, she did! Grinning, we checked in our luggage and headed off to the business class lounge, which was where my brain started squirming and the pretence began. *You don't belong here!* it shouted. *Everyone else does, look at them, they know what to do. You're a scruffy backpacker, they can all tell.* Yeah, my brain thinks I'm trailer trash and wants to keep me in my place. But in this scenario I had no idea if I was supposed to start a tab, pay for the food and drinks on display or if they were free (yes, they're free). You don't need an explanation if you've experienced this before, been shown the ropes or maybe booked the proper way and received guidance. I felt fully undeserving because we hadn't paid (and therefore I shouldn't take anything extra?). By this point my husband had spotted a big screen with sports and, coffee and muffin in hand, migrated towards it. He'd found his comfortable place. I was less settled.

On the plane our flight attendant, Robert, asked what I'd like to drink. An orange juice please, I said. "Not wine? Bubbles? Are you sure?" After a couple of moments he established this was our first time in the fancy section of the plane and set about making sure we made the most of our experience. "Go on, have some champagne, it's free and all part of the service". Relieved I wouldn't blow my Canadian budget on the inflight refreshments, I gratefully accepted and sipped the golden bubbles, starting to relax. No need to pretend anymore, he knows we haven't been here before and he's ok with it. More than ok, as Robert now considered it his personal mission to make damn sure we made the most of it! By the time our food came out served on china plates instead of a plastic tray, and the seats reclined into a bed, I was ready to enjoy every minute of the experience.

Some people will make the most of a luxury experience if presented with an opportunity, and I try really hard to be one of them. But usually I'm firmly in the group of those who need to understand the parameters and expectations before beginning to feel comfortable in the new scenario.

If you've ever been in situations above your paygrade (according to your asshat of a brain, that is), you'll recognise that slightly uncomfortable feeling I'm talking about. It's like having a new pair of shoes you bought to look ultra professional at a business event but they haven't been broken in, so after a couple of hours you're spending all your time trying to persuade your face to appear relaxed while ignoring the pain emanating throughout your whole body.

This scenario also plays into your business and marketing.

Anxious about success

Those pesky mind gremlins are throwing up new barriers and ever-changing goal posts to keep you safe. Each time you discover a new piece of information about your potential clients, a mind gremlin will add that to the folder and suggest a new reason why you aren't ready. It's too big a jump from where you are now! Stay home! Stay safe!

Let's look at the example of pricing. You *know* that when you're working for a translation agency, the end client pays your rate plus the proofreader plus the agency's margin to cover their work and overheads. But you associate your translation work with the rate you charge the agency. If you're being paid x cents a word for excellent translation, you ask yourself how you could confidently charge triple that for the same work? Yes, you're working with a reviser and paying them and you have to market yourself, liaise with the client etc. But logic aside, you associate that translation you produced with a certain rate and a big jump doesn't feel possible or somehow makes you feel like you're overcharging the client.

It doesn't help that you're constantly being bombarded with conversations about falling rates, the dire state of the industry and how you've seen colleagues struggle to make ends meet and leave the profession. Why should you be the one to do well? Your mind gremlins will absorb all these negative facts and produce a 50-page slide presentation listing all the reasons why you should 'stay in your lane'.

If you've ever used the phrase 'I got lucky' when you landed a lucrative project or new client then you could well be devaluing your hard work and effort. It's hard to believe *you* made it happen if it felt like the project came to you easily. First, not everything has to be hard and second, take the win! You did the background work by putting yourself out there, you networked, created a website, attended a conference, asked the right questions, did a good job on previous projects and got a referral. You played a huge part in making that 'luck' come about.

Your happy place?

Do these character traits sound familiar?

- Perfectionism i.e. setting unrealistic expectations and judging yourself harshly when you don't achieve them 100%

- A quest to achieve expert status – feeling like you never have enough knowledge, you need to learn more, prepare more, gain further qualifications etc. (there's never an end, you know)

- An attempt to become a Super Freelancer, making yourself indispensable. In other words, working until you're close to burnout, wanting to please everyone so that clients are sure to return

These traits are all related to not feeling like you're good enough or deserving of those higher-end clients.

If any of this sounds just a tad familiar, you may well push back against my insistence that you can go out there right now and claim everything you want and more. You'll select a few 'facts' as presented by your mind gremlins, who are readily prepared with mountains of evidence. How do I know? Because I also have more than a few mind gremlins that need keeping in check.

When external validation isn't enough

Whatever I tell you isn't going to be enough. You can have a whole team of people cheering you on from the sidelines, happy clients and colleagues who know you have the translation skills, language and subject knowledge to charge higher rates for the next tier of clients. And while you might take a moment to bask in the glory of all that positivity, the idea that you're good enough will still seem faintly absurd. Other people might be fooled, but you know the "truth". They can give you a bullet-proof list of reasons to prove what they're saying and you'll still find reasons to dismiss them. Far be it for you to be remotely like those translation agencies who promise all languages for all specialist fields regardless of their actual expertise. Avoiding that level of confidence means you veer towards the other extreme of not promising anything that you can't do standing on your head.

The perfect level of confidence is just enough to reassure the client you are the best choice for their next project, but not so much that you feel uncomfortable proclaiming your abilities.

If you're the type of person who has no issue with doubling their rates tomorrow, just because someone said it was a good idea, then you're probably not reading this book. But if that does describe you, please bottle that self-belief and share some with the rest of us!

For me, transitioning my business is always more about gradually building up and generating the evidence (for myself) over time. I suspect you might be similar. You might feel you have to get another higher qualification – no! That's unlikely to be the case. I bet you're already working on the types of texts you would translate for direct clients. It might be fun to take another course (and I also love learning) but do it *in addition to* taking marketing action rather than before you start.

Here are a few practical ways to prove to yourself that your skills and knowledge justify the next step – even if you're a non-believer:

- Find a mentor (often at a very low cost within association networks). A mentor is someone who is further along in their career and specialised in an area you want to work in. They may assign you a translation project and provide feedback on your work. You can ask questions and receive experienced advice. If you're confident in your translation skills then maybe search for a mentor outside of the translation industry for business mentoring, which you can usually find locally.

- Work with a colleague and pay them to revise your translations – you'll learn from them and/or get feedback that your work is already good enough. And as a handy bonus, the fact you're paying them means you have to charge more to the end client. It's often easier to justify a higher rate when others are involved than if you're the sole beneficiary. I'd recommend working as a translator + reviser pair anyway when translating for direct clients because you'll get a far better outcome and your reviser will read your translation with fresh eyes – suggesting translation solutions you might not have considered and spotting typos etc. If they're further along in their business and work with direct clients already, they'll also act as a mentor if you explain that you're open to honest feedback and advice. There are benefits to both parties: you're generating work for them by paying your colleague to revise your translations and if you work together well, they're likely to repay the favour and refer suitable projects to you in the future.

- Ease yourself into a new situation and create the proof you need. Take a micro-step towards your goals. This might involve increasing your fee for the next translation. It might be lurking in a forum to read what your prospective clients are saying about their industry. It might be making an enquiry about contributing an article to an industry magazine.

Incremental steps

Over time I've become more comfortable with paying more and expecting to pay more for various services. Translation is a profession you can theoretically start on a shoestring. With just internet access and basic software, you're good to go. Ideally, you'd be better equipped, maybe with membership of a professional association, a website and an email address with your custom domain. Further down the road, you'll add some costlier software, pay for an accountant or gain help with other aspects of your business. You build up gradually, as does your comfort level and expectation of valuable products and services. The more you pay, the higher your expectation of the outcome – which is exactly the belief you're projecting about the quality of your own service and debating whether you can meet your clients' high expectations. But, at some level, this elevated service is just packaging. You're paying more for convenience, top customer service and those special extra touches on top of the service or product you're buying.

We've all learnt another language. At first, the words look completely alien. You start learning the sounds and might be able to pronounce some words without knowing what they mean. Then you add meaning and context. Then before you know it, you're in Bavaria having studied German for the past 9 years and realise you're smack bang in the homelands of a whole new dialect, and language learning has taken on an unexpected twist.[1] It takes time to acclimatise to daunting differences in culture, climate, and dialect and it's the same when making progress with business goals. You build up confidence over time, easing yourself in gradually.

---

1. I may not have earned my Bavarian Dirndl dress but by the end of a year in Regensburg I could at least throw in a convincing "An Guadn" (Guten Appetit) and "schau ma moi" (let's see) with the best of them.

I don't want you to lower your expectations about what's possible but I do want you to feel okay with it taking a little time. And because it's going to take time, you may as well get started now, right?

Action

If I referred you to a dream client, what would stop you being excited about that?

Write down those concerns as you play out that scenario in your mind and see if there's any evidence you need to gather to prove to yourself that you can feel more comfortable working with a higher level of client.

Then, brainstorm how you could go about getting that evidence while marketing your services – rather than before you start.

Example

My mindset gremlins popped up recently when one of my translation clients asked my opinion of a new product name. They wanted to pay me for the time spent discussing various name options as a native speaker.

Instantly I assumed they wanted me to come up with new creative suggestions on the spot – not part of my normal service and not a skill of mine, especially when unfamiliar with the new product they were creating (this was a new direction for the company). My brain went to "*Imposter! You can't charge for your opinion when you don't know what you're talking about. What are the legal ramifications if you suggest something that already has a trade mark? What if they make a terrible decision based on your opinion?*"

Wow, that was a big leap from a simple question!
After clarifying the brief, I discovered my client simply wanted an English speaker's initial reaction to a product name and to understand any positive or negative associations I would make based on the name. They expected to throw a few different examples at me, so knew this would take a little time. They needed this extra evidence to present to their shareholders, who would agree the shortlist, and then everything would go through the legal team etc. for checks and whatever else is involved. Not the big daunting task I wrongly assumed and perfectly within my capabilities. If I needed a second opinion, I have colleagues and a British husband who could help with this particular question.

If you're reading this example and shaking your head at the ridiculousness of it all, that's fine by me. We all have these moments! Often, clarifying what's actually needed will show us that we can comfortably deliver what's needed and have us questioning why we waited so long to go after those higher-level clients/projects/opportunities. Hindsight is a wonderful thing.

* * *

Now you know you can acclimatise yourself gradually to next-level clients, let's talk about your motivation to reach that destination.

Chapter 2

Why Motivation Is A Poor Travel Companion

The freedom to explore at our own pace and head off the main tourist trail was our goal in New Zealand. Julia and I decided to hire a shiny white Suzuki Esteem as our wheels for five weeks, which was a bargain at NZ$ 15 a day. The only minor problem, Scotty the car dealer told us, was that the petrol gauge was broken so best top the car up with fuel sharpish and keep an eye on the mileage. Despite visions of us running on empty and being stranded in the middle of nowhere, confounded by our questionable map reading skills (this was the days before satnav and cheap smartphones) we kept a close eye and written record of our mileage, making it from Auckland to Christchurch without too many close calls.

Our motivation to hire a cheap car was the quest for freedom and the power to choose our own adventure as new and exciting places took our fancy. That's the kind of motivation that pulls you forward and gives you an incentive to take action. But it's not the only kind. You've probably also experienced external motivation to avoid a situation – in our case, the determination to not find ourselves stranded without petrol. But we also wanted to avoid splurging our tight budget on something as unnecessary as a fully functioning car, leaving more for fun adventures and wine. And, of course, to avoid travelling on the Big Green Backpacker Party Bus, which was as appealing as another week in the cockroach-infested hostel we left behind in Kings Cross, Sydney. When you look at it like that, negative and positive motivation can be equally compelling.

Let's talk about why you're reading this book and your motivation to make a change.

We'll start with the negatives: You might be sick to the back teeth of working endless hours for a relatively modest income. You feel forced to make a change because of downward price pressures or new advances in machine translation and artificial intelligence that have increased post-editing requests and decreased the satisfaction you derive from translation projects. Your favourite agency clients may have been taken over and switched to automatic project notification. Now the requests get sent out to a raft of translators and no matter how trigger happy you are, the job has gone a few seconds before you can read the filename, let alone open the file.

Sometimes life just changes: Perhaps you have new family or health commitments limiting your available time, and you need to earn more in fewer hours. Or maybe you're more available than you used to be and you're ready to commit to finding direct clients without worrying about publicising part-time hours or outsourcing to meet deadlines.

The Big Dream: You desperately want less hassle, a higher income, greater job satisfaction. You might want to put your kids through college without crippling debt or pay off your mortgage. Even more exciting, you have incredible travel plans, would love a new home office in the garden, a fancy car. Maybe you have your sights set on projects to make the world a better place but they all require time and money you just don't have.

Your motivation (and mine) is a faulty fuel gauge to keep an eye on but mostly work around

Common wisdom suggests that the Big Dream is what will keep you going when life gets tough. It will pull you through, and in times of doubt just dream bigger. Make it enticing! Create colourful reminders and vision boards so your eye's always on the prize. Does that really work for you? No, me neither. I do believe it's important to get clear about what you truly want and to start taking small steps to put those plans into action, but the big dream isn't a good enough motivator on a daily basis.

I was once sold on the idea that a compelling goal was all you needed to provide endless motivation. I thought the reason I wasn't achieving my goals was because my dream wasn't compelling enough. How's that for double bashing yourself? You're failing to meet the goals you've set yourself and now your dream isn't good enough?! I dug deep into visualising my ideal lifestyle, the big travelling trip I wanted to take, all that extra time I'd spend with family and friends, all the languages and skills I want to learn etc. And it still wasn't enough because – and let's see if this is the same for you – the specific goals I had were too far removed from my current reality. They simply gave me the excuse to congratulate myself on my current set-up. *Oh, I've managed in far worse situations so where I am now is fine, that dream trip can be done another year. What's relevant to me right now is the income I need to earn to pay the next bill / do a specific training / pay for a surprise car breakdown* [insert your own pressing financial commitment].

Some days you wake up and your positivity has done a runner and taken your mojo with it. Your cat jumps at the loud groan you release from behind your screen as you resign yourself to the uninspiring enquiries in your inbox, which not even a double shot of espresso can pep up. Where's motivation when you need it?

Like that faulty fuel gauge, motivation can't be trusted. Here are a few hard truths:

1. Motivation is unreliable. **It's inconsistent** and goes up and down depending on your mood, energy, and whether the wind is blowing from an easterly or southerly direction.

2. **It can actually lead to inaction.** Wait, what?! You wait for motivation to strike, because you think you need it to take action. And while you're waiting, your goals are getting further away, dragging your mojo further down.

3. You **burn up all your motivation** on other tasks, leaving nothing in the tank for marketing and other business-boosting activities. If you've ever set yourself a daily or weekly marketing goal, only to let that slide off your list, one reason may have been that you packed your day full with translation and other tasks. At the end of a busy day you've got no energy left to do something you might be dreading anyway.

4. Your big dreams can be **so far away they actually become demoralising**. This one resonates strongly with me (see compelling goal above).

5. Motivation needs clarity. You can't be motivated if you're **not clear** about what you need to do, and even

what you want to avoid. Perhaps something is holding you back, but you haven't uncovered exactly what that something is and you can't jump over a hurdle you can't see. Sometimes the problem is not understanding the connection between your current actions and the ultimate goal. If that's the case then you might convince yourself that your current task is a pointless exercise and waste of time, especially when your energy is low.

So if we can't rely on motivation to kickstart our marketing, what can we do?

What really motivates us?

Making progress. Gaining momentum. Taking action. Even if it's the last thing you feel like doing, try to take the tiniest of teeny micro-steps because on these days the sense of accomplishment will be even greater.

And when you do take those steps, acknowledge and celebrate those wins. This gives you a little dopamine hit, with the added bonus that you then associate your task with positivity, giving you an extra dose of encouragement to keep going. Use brain chemistry to your advantage!

We're very bad at not celebrating the little steps we've taken because it doesn't feel like we've achieved anything. Take Ken,[1] for example. He was clear about his target clients and had created a list of companies that looked interesting. He went about phoning a few to discuss possibilities and find out more about them, and came away with four interested contacts. That's more than a little step, in fact that's a giant leap for many of us, but because they weren't clients at that point, he didn't consider that a win. A colleague quite rightly stopped him and pointed out the progress he'd made and that many of us would consider picking up the phone and calling even one potential client nothing short of miraculous.

You make progress through momentum, from taking a series of little steps, sometimes so small you can barely detect the difference. Over time you'll be a long way further down the road than you could have imagined and will likely have built up momentum from your first barely there micro-steps to taking longer, more purposeful strides.

Getting closer to your goals

When you start working with your first direct client after years of working with agencies, it's like you've opened the vault and a

---

1. Kenneth Beattie, architect and translator who you can find at www.kennword.com

whole load of possibilities come flying out. That first direct client or high-paying project proves to you that it's possible. It validates your efforts, and you get a taste of what's possible, spurring you on to find even more.

Do you remember your first translation project? Even if that was a good many years back you can imagine how it felt to send that translation off, then your invoice, and see the payment come in your bank account. You've already taken so many steps towards your bigger business goals, you got your second client, third, fourth, fifth... raised your rates, set some boundaries. We're just building on these steps and exploring different routes. You took a long break in the middle? No problem! Now you're ready to start the next part of your journey, one step at a time.

Action

What have you been putting off that you could spend 5 minutes on right now? Maybe it's business related or maybe it's just something you want to do for no obvious reason. Whatever it is, take 5 minutes and do something towards it. I'll wait.

Example

"Get my portfolio done" became a constant presence on my to-do list. If a task keeps getting moved, then you want to figure out why. So I asked myself:

Does it need to get done – can I delegate or delete it?
I could drop it entirely but it's something I want to do, at least one client has asked for it before and it's a good marketing tool. I can't delegate this unless I provide at least the basic content.

Sounds like the motivation is there, so why is it not getting done?
The word 'portfolio' makes it sound like a mammoth task; the workload is unclear because it could become anything from a one-page profile to a 20-page booklet, and then should it be a slide presentation, or be hosted on my website? Will it contain translation samples or case studies? Is it for all my clients or focused on one specific field? There are too many questions to answer before I start.

In that case, can I flip the task and work backwards?
That could work. What do I have already that I can use? From my website I have specific copy e.g. for chemical coatings clients. I have a couple of different projects I could use for case studies and testimonials in this field. I have content on my about page and from sales letters I've created. Now I know I have content, I'm excited to find a template on Canva and see what I can create. If I get stuck, I can ask the website company I work with or a graphic

designer colleague to help out. Oooh! That feels much easier and I've got the next steps clear now.

If you find you're prolonging a task, try asking yourself questions about where the friction lies: does it need to be done now, by you or not at all? Dig into where the hard part is and try tackling it from a different angle.

The friction you identify could be your brain trying to take you on a dastardly detour.

Chapter 3

The Dastardly Detours Of Your Brain

Landing in Tokyo, disorientated from jet lag and general excitement, we made our way to Shinjuku to meet our patient and generous Japanese host, Emi. As soon as we met, out poured a flood of fast-spoken French. "Wait one hot second!", my brain cried, did we just get on an 11-hour Eurostar train to Paris by mistake? And if so, where were my croissants?

Julia had met Emi on their year abroad in Limoges, France, and so they were used to speaking French together. I'd studied French up to the age of 19 so can just about get by and so we spent our time in Japan: With Julia and Emi speaking French, and me translating the gist in English to my cousin, Simon, woefully inadequately at times. And then hearing and being confronted with symbols and actions that definitely weren't covered in our Tricolore French textbook or any other language lesson I'd attended.

By the end of the 10 days my brain had done enough mental gymnastics to avoid any cultural faux pas, learn a few words of Japanese, understand that the meaning of certain actions was undoubtedly the opposite of my initial thought, and feel my way a little bit rather than expecting everything to instantly make sense. Just when I thought I'd cracked it, I bit into what I soon discovered to be an octopus dumpling and realised that little yellow van we discovered two days earlier had either changed the menu or I'd misunderstood once again.

Your brain can cope with all kinds of complicated mental pathways to help you figure things out. But, it turns out, not all of them are helpful. When it comes to marketing and other business tasks we're not excited about, your mind can take you on some dastardly detours that prevent you getting started and eat into your time.

Your time is precious

One of the biggest objections any small business owner has when it comes to marketing is time. We're all focused on generating income from client work to pay the bills, naturally, and baulk at spending large chunks of unpaid time working on our business. Common practical solutions include outsourcing tasks to get more done in the same time – even if you have the skill to do it yourself – because you can then focus on client work and make time for other projects. Another option is to hire a guide and get help from someone more experienced who knows how to get you where you need to go. It moves you along more quickly and gives you confidence that you are taking the right next step. BUT those options need financial investment that you might not be willing or able to pay. It's a catch 22.

You don't have the time to market but...
→ You want to work with higher-paying clients
→ You need to do marketing to attract those clients
→ But you don't have the time
→ You haven't got the budget to pay for help
→ So you'll have to do it yourself
→ And we're back to you not having the time again.

One thing to avoid when your time is limited is taking an unnecessary detour, so let's take a look at some common issues and make sure we know how to avoid them.

Dastardly Detours Level 1: The scenic route

Yes, the scenic route may be pretty, but it may also take you further out of your way. These detours might entice you when you pick a marketing activity that you think you *should* do, but when it comes to getting started your chosen activity is too daunting, unappealing or takes too much time.

Procrasti-training?

If a task is too daunting, we will break open our never-ending list of procrastination activities. We procrastinate for various reasons – sometimes because we need a break and are overwhelmed, anxious, tired, or have no energy. Sometimes, it's because we've decided to do this thing called marketing and we're not really clear on what we have to do. Instead of coming up with a plan, we attend a training session (or another perfectly useful distraction) and the host will nicely lay out how to spend your time. Simply join the Zoom room at the relevant time or catch the replay later. Click play, sip a warm beverage and make the odd note or comment to contribute. Useful skill learnt – tick, Marketing action taken – 0.

Just out of reach

If you find yourself with no energy to spend on marketing yourself, it might be because you find it boring or you think it's too big. You may be working all day on client work to earn the money you need, so once you've finished for the day the last thing you feel like doing is working on your business. Even if you set aside some protected time at the end of the week or when your client work is done, it's rare you won't encroach on that time when work expands, an urgent request rears its head or you decide you'd rather get ahead on next week's work because it's going to be busy. If it sounds like I've been staking out your office and applying my mind-reading talents to hear your thoughts, then I'd suggest setting up a better home surveillance system.

Only joking. It's because those are my default behaviours too. It's so easy to push anything other than client work to the bottom of the pile and find yourself only delving into marketing activities during random and unstructured slow periods.

Treadmill to nowhere
Translators frequently tell me they want to do marketing but can never find the time. *I just need to finish this project and then I'll set aside some time for marketing.* If this sounds familiar, ask yourself whether you find the time for an interesting webinar or fun activity. Please don't think I'm trying to shame anyone or encouraging you to make time despite there only being so many hours in the day. I definitely don't advocate getting up at 4 am, adding an extra two days to your working week or forcing yourself to sit at your desk for hours on end to get everything done. That's not appealing in the slightest!

What I am saying is that we tend to find the time for activities we enjoy, those that are fun, easy and appealing in some way. And that's what I want you to tap into. How can you make marketing easier and more appealing to you?

Time-bending possibilities to get you back on track

If you think I'm going to start talking productivity hacks, prepare to be disappointed. Marketing struggles rarely have much to do with time. You will always make time for a fun activity, or one that grabs your attention, over less exciting tasks. So let's start by making marketing more exciting.

- **Choose your own adventure:** Imagine you're flicking through a travel brochure and feeling inspired by the visuals of lush rainforests, sparkling waterfalls and the calls of exotic birds. Or perhaps you've got your eye on a boutique hideaway where you can marvel at the spectacular scenery while relaxing in an oasis of peace and tranquility. That's your chosen destination and the smaller hassles such as updating your passport, packing, and booking a house or petsitter feel insignificant when the prize is so appealing. My aim with this book is to make marketing feel easier and more enjoyable so look out for the tips coming your way in the next few chapters.

- **Travel light, go further:** Find low-energy tasks that you can do in small pockets of time even when you're not feeling the vibe. Small steps feel easier and will ensure you keep making progress. Even big marketing projects are manageable when you break them down and know your next step. You'll have more energy when the destination is clearly what you want and you can see yourself making progress towards that goal. We covered motivation in Chapter 3, so I'll just say here that creating some forward momentum is key and while you might need to take a few uphill strides initially, a lighter burden (whether that's a lighter mental burden or a smaller physical to-do list) will soon have you heading back downhill as you build up speed without trying, racing down that mountain for your sundowner refreshment. Mine's a frozen strawberry daiquiri, cheers!

- **Send your brain on a trip:** Gamify the process: If your brain believes an activity is easy, you'll feel it in your bones, so let's play a Jedi mind trick. Set a timer for ten minutes and tick off a small marketing task. Keep a list of these types of tasks ready for when you're short of time and pick one to complete against the clock. These could range from sending a connection request to a potential client on LinkedIn or commenting on an interesting post. Pick one company you would like to work with and add it to a campaign list for the future. Ask a client for a testimonial / referral / introduction to like-minded people.

Make marketing even more fun by creating a bingo card with small tasks you want to complete and choose a reward to enjoy when you've ticked off the squares. I used a program called Atticus to write this book and set a goal to write 500 words a day, Monday to Friday. The program recorded my progress and I really wanted that fire emoji and green square on its calendar every day. The words weren't the end result and many were edited out later, but it gave me an easy game to play when I told myself I was uninspired.

Hopefully, these suggestions offer a few ways of 'bending' time and show you that marketing is a tad more manageable (and you're possibly already doing it). However, these are all tactics – extremely useful tips and tricks to break down bigger goals and make the workload easier. All the same, I suspect there might still be some reticence to putting yourself out there and exploring new client collaboration possibilities and that can be explained by Dastardly Detours Level 2. These little gremlins masquerade as proof that you can't take action and need to hold back a little longer.

Dastardly Detours Level 2
(a.k.a. more substantial barriers in the way of you reaching those awesome clients)

Since the dawn of time, translators (including past me) have cited a long list of reasons stopping them marketing to direct clients. All are problems that absolutely must be solved before actual marketing can start. These include 'facts' such as you aren't specialised enough or don't know enough, as well as worries about screwing up your approach and ruining your future chances with a dream client. You're concerned about your rusty second language skills, which mean you won't be able to impress potential clients, and you don't know what challenges your potential clients face so have no idea how you can add value. Some translators tell me they might not be able to handle the demands because they don't have fancy software, aren't available 24/7 or have some other entirely logical problem.

If I asked you to provide evidence of such barriers, I'm certain you would find irrefutable proof. However, that doesn't mean that you can't, or shouldn't, market like you mean it.

There will always be more specialist knowledge to learn, language skills to maintain or improve, and insights to gain into what your clients need and want that will change from person to person and from day to day. Gaining extra qualifications, getting regular practice in your second language, perfecting your sales technique ready for the next step and researching all the different aspects of your potential clients' business for hours on end will only reveal more 'gaps' and barriers to starting. Even people who have industry experience and switch to translation as a second career will soon find their experience-based knowledge out of date as technology moves on.

When these concerns arise, explore the following questions to decide if you really need to go on that destructuve detour.

1. **Is your concern true?** For example, are your spoken

language skills as rusty as you believe?

2. **What positive factors are also true?** For example, your spoken language skills may be rusty. But it is also true that you write in that language regularly, and you can ask a colleague to check or even translate your initial emails, sales letters and other marketing. It is probably also true that you have clients with whom you've never spoken in person. It is also true that you can get spoken language practice to build your communication skills in your second language while marketing at the same time.

Often, your answer to question one may be a resolute 'Yes!' as you scramble to collect the proof to support your argument. The second question may take a little more thought, but approach it from the perspective of 'What is also true that would mean I could take action and make progress right now?'.

Action

What's one way your brain takes you on a dastardly detour? Note it down and explore if your concerns are actually true and which positive factors also apply.

Example

Concern: I told myself that I couldn't run a direct response marketing campaign because I didn't have time to contact 100 potential clients (which is the minimum number quoted in all the advice I've seen given by marketing professionals).

Was this true? H*mmm, partially. It was probably more about not wanting to make the time to contact so many people because that felt overwhelming. "It's too many for me to keep track of if I carry out the campaign the way I want to do it (personalised, making an offer that takes time to deliver, no complicated software systems etc.)."*

What positive factors did I decide were true? *I can make the time for a smaller-scale project and carry out the campaign the way I want for a smaller number of people. There's that one client I gained by consistently keeping in touch and making them offers, and I've gained clients from contacting 10 people at a time. I have a lot of material ready to be adapted so it won't take as long as I thought. The minimum result would be new contacts, the best result could be multiple new clients.*

* * *

Next up: How to make a molehill out of a mountain. Let's go!

Chapter 4

Marketing – The Mountainous Megabeast Rears Its Head...

And Lets Out A Friendly Squeak

Not all mountains require a survival kit, near-death experiences, altitude sickness and years of vigorous training.

But many people associate the word 'marketing' with that kind of torture. If that's you, you might end up sticking to an easier trail around the bottom of the mountain, tweaking the phrasing on your website or posting on social media. The idea of creating a marketing campaign or even contacting a single dream client with a plan to follow up and keep in touch is too much to contemplate. Instead this gets pushed to the side as one of those Things That Would Be Nice To Do but you honestly don't have the time or energy to climb a mountain right now, thank you very much.

The good news is that there are some mountains you can climb without an experienced guide. You just need some trainers, a basic level of fitness, and a daypack with some water and snacks. You could even choose to take the cable car and make use of the toilet facilities when you reach the summit.

Table mountain in Cape Town, South Africa, isn't Everest and you can scale the summit and be back in time for dinner the same day. Incredibly, there is usually a cable car to take you up the mountain, and a cafe at the top! However, the cable car was broken and the cafe closed when I visited, which meant that my travel companions and I had the magnificent views mostly to ourselves and fewer people around encouraged the rock rabbits (or dassies) to come out and play. Reaching the summit involved some mild rock climbing, minimal shade, and a particularly steep section through a narrow gorge – but also the opportunity to cool off a little under a natural waterfall and admire the stunning scenery along the way. We hiked up at a moderate pace, the word mountain is in its name and that's good enough for me, I'm claiming it – I climbed a mountain!

The route back down would have taken longer had we not listened to a local. Bluntly informed that we shouldn't consider our chosen route through the botanical gardens if we don't know the area and definitely wouldn't make it before sundown, we carried on undeterred. Were we not brave explorers and clearly more capable than that experienced hiker suspected? A little while later we didn't appear to be any closer and begrudgingly cast our ego aside. Retracing our steps to the summit (does that mean I climbed a mountain twice?), we picked the quicker route as directed and reached the bottom 90 minutes later. Despite having climbed glaciers and kayaked, cycled and trekked our way around in the previous months, my muscles had plenty to say about their treatment the next morning so as a workout, the 'easy' mountain hike was still a decent physical challenge.

Just because a challenge is easier than you think it should be, it doesn't mean it's any less impressive or that it won't get you the same results. There's no need to kill yourself or make a challenge harder than it needs to be because you want to reach peak accomplishment. That's your ego talking and those 'no pain, no gain' messages that get touted about. Your sneaky subconscious needs to believe it can't be that easy because otherwise you would have done it before... wouldn't you? Well, if we're talking about marketing now, I suspect you already are doing a little bit of marketing here and there.

What is marketing anyway?

Every time you talk to someone, post on social media, interact in any way, you are marketing yourself. Someone else is listening to you, reading your words or seeing your actions and receiving some kind of message about you. They won't have the full story but they've formed an opinion, however vague. Marketing is having conversations, making connections, building relationships, and getting to know people.

It's when we look at marketing as that thing we must do to win over people and grow our business that it suddenly becomes a mountainous marketing beast breathing down our neck. One of the reasons marketing used to scare me is that I wouldn't naturally meet the people I wanted to work with. I don't live in the same country as most of my clients and so it was unlikely I'd meet my future clients out and about in the UK. With young children, I couldn't and didn't want to travel regularly so when I did, it needed to count. This meant I had to put myself in uncomfortable situations and then felt I needed to be the most highly polished business person exuding brilliance with every word. And that's just not me. I might stumble over my words, make the odd joke, and struggle to hold a conversation while eating/drinking and trying not to drop any number of things about my person (if you ever meet the person who thought standing breakfast buffets to network was a good idea, please let me know. I need to have a word).

Tame the mountainous marketing megabeast

How did I slay that particular marketing beast? Initially, by spending a little time figuring out what exactly I didn't like and what I wished would be easier, and then looking at what might be possible within that framework.

My list of requirements included the following.

1. Long-distance relationship: I realised I wanted a more regular form of marketing I could do from a distance without travel time or expense.

2. Reduce the pressure: I wanted to take the pressure off the occasions when I did travel and attend events but still come away feeling accomplished with new contacts.

3. Structure: I needed to get clear on how I could turn marketing into a project with defined tasks to work my way through. Ideally, also with deadlines because that works well with my client work.

4. Greater control: Search engine optimisation and social media posting has its place but I wanted greater control over who sees my marketing. I wanted to get short-term feedback to know if a type of marketing is resonating with my target market, whether it is effective or not, so I could adapt if needed.

5. Small pockets of time: Ideally, I needed to break down any big projects into bite-sized pieces and find smaller activities I could fit into a busy lifestyle.

If you've been intimidated by the concept of marketing, you might breathe easier knowing you don't have to follow a prescribed route. You can absolutely adapt, mix and match, and find a way that works best for you right now.

Over time, your life and situation will change – you might have children or other caring responsibilities, take on a major home renovation project, your children might head off on their own adventures giving you more time to focus on work (or you might not want to spend all that time on translation). Or you might be location independent.

At any point in your life or future plans, your business and marketing will need to adapt and it absolutely can. There is no one-size-fits-all strategy, only individual versions of the key marketing principle: Taking action to engage with and attract your target audience with the ultimate aim of increasing sales a.k.a. your income.

Action

If you could wave a magic wand and design the perfect type of marketing for you, what requirements would you have?

Start with what you absolutely don't want and can't do because that's usually clear in your mind, and then include all those reasons you would list for not marketing proactively now or in the past. Then write down what you are willing to do and make this a positive list of requirements.

Example

- I want a plan and actions I can follow
- Quick feedback to know if I'm on the right track
- Deadlines to keep me consistent
- Something I can do from home without relying on events
- But I do still like to travel and go to events so maybe incorporate the odd one somehow – yes I want it all!

This is how I decided to start contacting clients directly in a structured marketing campaign. I got more or less instant feedback in the responses (although no response was also feedback), I planned out when I would send emails and sales letters, and how I'd follow up with dates. Attending an event could be one of the contact points in my campaign, but if I couldn't attend it still gave me a focused date to work towards.

* * *

Even if you can't determine what type of marketing best fits your needs, note down your ideal requirements. It's absolutely fine to not know how everything fits together at first. With that in mind, we're off to explore the Great Unknown!

Chapter 5

The Great Unknown

Venturing out into The Great Unknown sounds exciting when flicking through a travel brochure or starting to learn a new language. You're off to explore new frontiers and feel a huge sense of freedom, discovering the secret treasures of a new place off the beaten track. That freedom is empowering and, if you're anything like me, you'll pick a location you've never been to before precisely because you know so little about it. You can't wait to explore the sights, sounds and tastes of a place that's completely different to your everyday surroundings.

Of course, when contemplating marketing options you aren't armed with a glossy travel brochure depicting fabulous direct client destinations and beckoning you to explore.

But if you had that brochure? It would be filled with epic scenery, picturesque views from office windows, photos of smiling people clinking glasses at networking events and dining out with happy clients in fabulous restaurants. The sun would always be shining.

There would be a choice of excursions to suit city slickers, beach lovers, adrenaline junkies, group or solo travellers, showing that there's a perfect destination for everyone.

***** Unbeatable value, takes you right to the heart of the action with all the support you need.

You'd be impressed by the well-thought out marketing itinerary. Days 1-3 would include a guided tour to 5 major client-rich locations with a local guide on hand to answer questions and smooth the way, providing cultural insights and advice. Each evening you would return to your boutique hotel with all the amenities you could wish for to rejuvenate after an invigorating day out.

***** Exceptional, knowledgeable service from friendly and helpful guides.

As well as lasting memories from your trip, you'd return home with souvenirs such as new business, contacts of people who would continue to sell on your behalf and real experience of how to market with ease. Information that you can put into practice over and over again, whenever you choose.

***** Wouldn't travel with anyone else. By far the best translator marketing experience out there!

Now, that sounds amazing, take my money this instant!

An unwelcome landscape

While that translator marketing experience brochure doesn't exist, you have probably come up with your own version. Except you might envisage a barren, grey landscape with murky swamps shrouded in fog and hidden dangers lurking around every corner. The hair on the back of your neck stands on end as you feel the locals' eyes on you, ready to pounce as you take a step in the wrong direction.

No wonder you have so little enthusiasm. The truth, as always, is somewhere inbetween the utopian travel brochure and the bleak and unwelcoming picture you've created.

While it's human nature for our brain to focus on the negative and keep us safe, as translators we're also trained to be professional nitpickers who zoom in on negative details. Translation itself is all about choosing just the right term to convey the perfect message. You analyse your work, read through, check again, find an error, check again sure that you must have missed something else – even a seemingly tiny slip-up like a misplaced comma – because you know it can make a difference, especially in technical texts. If you let a mistake slip through the net there could be financial penalties, you could lose business, upset a client and destroy your reputation for attention to detail. Perhaps. Next up you have a proofreader or reviewer whose sole job is to find the errors you missed or suggest another way to improve the phrasing. Your reasoning is called into question (or perhaps they're just asking out of sheer curiosity).

I'm not sure whether this industry trains us to be perfectionists or attracts those of us who set the highest standards for ourselves, never entirely satisfied with the results. It's a hazard of the profession but this critical eye we've developed also ruins our tolerance for uncertainty and our marketing mindset. It can even extend to a negative outlook in general, with many freelancers bemoaning the state of the industry. That's not you, I'm sure, but faced with this unwelcome landscape and an uncertain marketing outcome or new strategy, you'll likely devote even more time to research, consuming every scrap of information you can find. You try and prepare to the nth degree, working to uncover all the hidden obstacles and dangers you may encounter to ready yourself for the hard trek ahead.

Travel light, go further

Research is my jam too. I've invested lots of time and money on courses covering all kinds of topics related to marketing, sales and understanding my ideal client. A courageous translator on a quest for the information needed to craft the perfect marketing message that would have clients beating down my virtual door – but only if I could do it from behind my computer screen. I eventually discovered that the best training is hands on experience out in the field. And if you're in a rush to get the information you need because you're impatient for change, this is the quickest way too.

At this point you might be considering skipping over this section because it feels like a big jump from your cosy office life, but hear me out. There are different levels you can take according to your comfort zone and you can ease yourself forwards by taking small steps. Unless the idea excites you, don't think about launching into a sales conversation with your dream clients – your first step is simply to redirect and focus your research on the essential information for your next step. As an explorer, you can't always plan out the entire route before you know what the journey involves.

One casual conversation with someone in the queue for a coffee at an event can take you in a completely different direction to the one you envisaged. It could be a throwaway remark a client makes in an email or you spot a comment made by your target audience in a social media group and Bam! – your preconceived ideas are suddenly cast aside as you follow a more interesting trail that only the insiders know about. The secret route the locals keep to themselves, away from the tourists who don't know to look beyond the surface.

It starts with heading undercover, gradually building up to more proactive conversations:

Undercover sleuth: You listen in to conversations, watch event presentations by your target audience for your target audience. Gather market intelligence – a fancy way of saying collect details about your potential clients – by inhabiting their world, if only for small snippets of time. Take note of the topics they cover, the language they use, the way they present themselves and you'll gradually get a feel for what they really care about.

Curious tourist: You're ready to ask questions. There's no need to feel like an expert or to put on a 'Be More Professional' front, you're naturally interested in how their products and services work, where they're based, what exciting plans they have and want to talk about. I can't put my hand on my heart and say I'm always naturally interested in a pigment or machine that my potential clients are selling, but I am curious about the final applications and the challenges and opportunities in the global market. Ask your new contact's opinion about the best ways to keep up with the latest news, whatever… the goal is to find out more information and test if your theories and assumptions are true.

Intrepid explorer: You're ready to seek out the less-frequented route and don't care if the forecast is rain. Extend a friendly smile as you introduce yourself while digging into the reasoning behind the other person's answers. You want to know their challenges and their desires, what makes them tick and then see if you can find a match between your service and the outcome they want, gently exploring if it's worth you both discussing a collaboration.

Your experience is what matters

Your perspective isn't the same as mine. We likely work with different language pairs and for different industries. You'll have different restrictions and freedoms to me (though I'm all too familiar with limited budgets, working while bringing up two young children around my husband's random shift pattern and extended family commitments). And yes, someone out there will have worked with clients like those you seek and might be excellent at marketing. You excitedly ask them what they did, how they approached those clients etc. Some information may be useful but not all because another person, however similar they appear, will always have a different experience to you. You can't know what *you* think about a place until you're there, looking around for yourself. And it's the same with marketing and business.

No two journeys or perspectives are the same. And yet we can apply the same tools and techniques to get there, with a few tweaks and detours along the way. If I can ask you to do one thing, it's to keep an open mind and spend a little time exploring the possibilities before deciding that a route is not for you.

We think we need to know everything before taking action but it's *only by taking action* that we understand what we need to know. And it's ok that you don't know, because you can't. Taking action always trumps spending all your time on research and will accelerate your plans.

A thought for our clients

Bear in mind – your potential clients are also facing the Great Unknown by choosing to work with you. You're an unknown quantity often popping up out of the blue from a foreign country suggesting they work with you. They don't understand your qualifications, you don't have the bricks and mortar set-up of a larger company that might reassure them, and they might have received inferior translations in the past. Part of your job when marketing is to make it safe for your future clients to work with you, crafting a vision of how the partnership would work and the stunning results they can expect. Taking the pressure off yourself to explore the unknown may be easier if you switch the focus to your clients and how you can help them. I would never call you self-obsessed (how rude!), but if you're going to be obsessed by anything, let it be your clients – what makes them tick, what they need, and how they operate. It's a subtle shift in focus that has a huge impact on making the act of marketing feel much easier. And I'm all about making things easier as I hope you're getting to realise.

Action

Write this down in big letters: "It's Got To Be Me". Then stick it somewhere you can see as a reminder that you get to explore opportunities your way – but explore them you should.

Can you think of a time when you surpassed someone else's expectations? When I handed in my resignation and told my previous manager that I was setting up as a freelance translator, his response was "Oh? If you ever want to come back, there's a job here for you." Which was a lovely sentiment laced with a hint of "pfff, good luck making a go of that" – making me all the more determined to make a success of my new business!

* * *

Please don't rely on other people's opinions or perspectives as to whether a strategy, client or new set-up will work for you. Your requirements and plans are different to theirs. Life happens, plans change and there's always a way of adapting and refining our route. I've got you covered.

Chapter 6

Refining Your Route

No fewer than two steps into the rainforest and I stopped, possibly with a tiny squeal, as I came face to face with a gigantic web and its occupant, the golden orb spider. Assured they were harmless but disliking the proximity nonetheless, I edged around the trees and wondered whether us city-dwelling Brits might be better off following the road route to our destination instead of making our own way through the rainforest. What the hell, my friend and I decided, we were in the Daintree rainforest, a UNESCO world heritage site, and nature is all part of the experience. Having been unexpectedly startled from the outset, the '30-minute walk' took quite a bit longer as we stayed on high alert, listening to every noise, ducking around the spiders' webs, crossing a creek and finally arriving at a beautiful beach unscathed and all pretty much according to plan.

Except for the great big sign declaring that estuarine crocodiles inhabit this area. Just in case that wasn't enough, the sign also reminded us that *crocodile attack can cause serious injury or death.*

Hot, sweaty, and with the prospect of relaxing on this stunning coastline cruelly whipped away from us, our hearts sank. For a few minutes Julia and I scanned the horizon, unable to see any rogue reptiles and seriously considered settling down for a break anyway, away from the shore. But after seeing a 1m lizard run across our path before climbing up a tree, we remember where we are and take heed, finding the path that takes us to a car park where we can get a lift back to our hut in a camp called Crocodylus. Yes, the signs were there. Crocodylus. On the way back we also met a couple who had been kayaking around Snapper Island. Sometimes it takes a moment to put together all those tricky clues.

Sometimes you get disappointed and come to a dead end. With dismay, you think about all the effort you've put in to reach this point. It would have been nice to have seen "Danger Beach" labelled on the map but alas, we only found out after a hot and sweaty trek. Still, we flirted with danger and lived to tell the tale.

It's perfectly ok and usually preferable to readjust your route once you've received new information. You can always reject opportunities, but first get the information you need to make that decision.

Your destination isn't fixed. It can change, along with any stops along the way, at any time. Life takes a new turn, your business evolves, countries close their borders. Equally, you might reach your destination but not enjoy the surroundings as much as you had hoped. The dream client doesn't feel so ideal anymore. In which case I'd assess the situation and decide whether to adjust and adapt, or refer the client to a colleague and move on.

Outcome uncertain – when plans change

When you're out in the wild on an expedition, your plans can change with the weather, an injury, a forgotten piece of kit. You get creative with what's available. This applies at home too. A family member or pet get sick, you have a household emergency/repair to organise, or how about a positive example – your partner surprises you with a fabulous mini-break and you have to scramble to get the essentials sorted before you can go.

Knowing that you can cope with changing situations and deal with all kinds of circumstances gives you confidence in your abilities – can you transfer this resilience and inherent creativity to your business and marketing mindset?

You don't always know where you'll end up, or the route you'll take, until you start. You take action, gather information and base the next steps on the information you gather along the way.

We're all figuring it out as we go along

Business is all about making decisions under uncertainty. Linnea Gandhi and Erik Johnson, behavioural scientists and business researchers, wrote about this for the Harvard Business Review[1] and are in favour of an experimental approach to reduce that uncertainty (which I obviously love). They found that one problem with big businesses is that they only incentivise positive results. This deters employees from taking short-term risks that may not work, but may also bring unexpected and valuable insights to benefit the business in the long term.

As small businesses, your experiments and adventures carry a much lower risk and you're much more agile and able to adapt to new information. The personal approach you have as a solo business owner versus a major corporation is a huge advantage because you can talk directly to your target market and respond to any insights gleaned instantly.

If we take a look at uncertainty from the perspective of marketing, it may help to know that marketing professionals don't have it all figured out either. Marketing always has been part trial and error, part research-based stack the odds in your favour and part just give it a go and see what happens. One common practice used by marketing professionals is split testing, also known as A/B testing, where they try two different sales pitches for the product, service or message, to see which version works best. They run focus groups and carry out market research

---

1. https://hbr.org/2019/02/8-things-to-do-before-you-run-a-business-experiment

because all the qualifications and studies in the world cannot guarantee the one perfect message or strategy for a specific sector of people. If you look at it like this, who are we to think we can nail our message or marketing from the get go? Professionals are always testing, experimenting, exploring, so it makes sense to follow their example.

What we can control

Now I've explained that no one knows entirely what they're doing and that uncertainty is everywhere, let's look at what we can control. Our actions. Very often, we focus on the outcome – whether a potential client will say yes or no – instead of our process. Clients buy from us when *they're* ready, not when we're ready, so even if our message, service, and strategy are all perfectly aligned with those of our dream client, only a small number of people will actually be ready to collaborate when we contact them. We can set ourselves up for success though and focus on how many conversations we have, how many connections we make, what actions we're taking to be more visible in the right places and to the right people. If we're taking enough action (which we can track) then as a minimum we'll get the information we need to know if we're heading in the right direction and are more likely to achieve the results we want.

You can set yourself up for success by creating a fantastic product or service that you know is needed (and we absolutely know that translation is essential for international communication in its various guises). The details beyond merely providing translations are uncertain – for example who exactly your clients will be, the perfect message to express the value of your service and the texts you'll end up translating or editing. Marketing involves taking an educated guess, trying things out and gaining the insights you need to make any necessary changes. And marketing professionals are doing the same, there isn't one perfect strategy, technique or guaranteed outcome. Humans are messy and complex beings, and as we're marketing to other messy and complex humans, it stands to reason that we shouldn't expect the same results from repeating the same message each time. You can view this as exceedingly unhelpful or incredibly liberating, because it means that those marketing requirements you listed in Chapter 4 have just as much potential to work as anything else. As long as you are having conversations with the people you want to work with then you should be gathering the information you need to add a little more certainty and comfort to your approach.

Record your trail

Whether you're travelling into new territory or going over old ground, the best explorers keep a record of their trip. As well as providing exceptionally useful data, this helps in a few other ways:

- You know exactly what you've done, so you can retrace

your steps and do more of the same when it works out well.

- You'll be able to look back and see where your marketing went off course or your route needs refining – perhaps not all of it needs to be scrapped, you may just need a slight adjustment.

- It provides evidence for your brain. You might be telling yourself you're marketing and promoting yourself all the time because it feels like you are. Or you're berating yourself because it feels like you haven't done that much when you actually have a long list of mini-achievements to celebrate. Keeping a record provides indisputable facts to prove or disprove your assumptions.

Retrace your clients' route of discovery

Beyond your trail, do you know how your clients find you? That's equally important to record so you can determine which marketing route works well for your business. An easy way to do this if you have a contact form on your website is to add a field asking how they found you and to make it a routine question when you receive enquiries.

Action

What do you already track in your business?
How are you going to record your marketing trail?

Example

When I run a marketing campaign, I record names, dates and responses at every stage. I've got sales letters in English and German, emails I sent, photos of any physical packages and, importantly, figures on how many responses I received at the first point of contact, and also the second, third, fourth and fifth (if applicable). I know how many contacts became clients and my return on investment. After a few times running similar campaigns, I now know what to expect and can mix things up to gauge the impact and see if I can beat my past results.

I also track habits and weekly tasks in a simple tick box chart. I use this concept for short-term projects and find that ticking off daily progress towards a marketing goal builds momentum and keeps my focus on taking action.

This concept (and lots of other great tips for making progress towards your goals) is encouraged by James Clear in his book, Atomic Habits, which I highly recommend.

Chapter 7

The Journey To Yes Is Paved With Good Objections

The dolphins dart around me, over and under. I imagine them weaving an invisible rope cage that surrounds me, gradually pulling it tighter until I'm trapped. There are so many of them, and I find myself breathing rapidly, adrenaline coursing through my body as I listen intently for the horn to signal our return to the boat. At the same time I'm cursing myself – *everyone else is enjoying this, why don't you like it? It's a once-in-a-lifetime experience and you're not making the most of it, what's wrong with you?*

Swimming with dolphins was not all it's cracked up to be.

Kaikoura, in New Zealand's South Island, is known for its whale watching, but when I spotted that you could take a more active role and swim with seals or dolphins, I opted for the seals. Except it was the wrong season for seal trips, which is why the next day, still pitch black at 5 am, I stood on a boat shivering in a wetsuit, flippers and snorkel, ready to dive in with the wild dolphins. Plans change, right?

We spot the first pod of dusky dolphins and jump in the sea. They get curious and race over to us, swimming underneath, circling me and others. I didn't appreciate how huge these creatures are and how unique an experience it would be. The dolphins didn't get the "no touching" memo and, anxious not to break the rules, I spend more time trying to avoid them than swim with them. After a couple more tries, I finally admit it's not the fun experience people rave about – for me that is. The next opportunity to swim I stay on the boat, rejoice in the hot water being poured down my wetsuit and get changed. It suited me just fine to warm up with a hot chocolate and biscuits and take photos of the dolphins' antics from the boat.

Some experiences might not work for you. Some clients might not be right for you, or you might not be right for them. There could be a mismatch in rates, ways of working, personality clashes, unrealistic expectations on both sides with neither party wanting to change their position. There are countless factors with the potential to cause frustration or disappointment as you realise a business relationship, collaboration or dream project just isn't what you wanted. And that's ok.

A two-way street named rejection

Imagine you've finally started chatting to one of your dream clients and they're interested in collaborating. But after a few conversations you feel a little uneasy about their budget expectations or the way they insist on working with a translation partner. You're open to exploring different options but they're not willing to bend. Perhaps you just don't vibe with the other party. You can reject them too, even if you're the person who made the first contact. As long as you've gathered the information you need to make an informed decision and aren't just writing them off based on the contents of their website, you're perfectly entitled to tell them you're not a good fit and offer a recommendation for a different translation provider if you wish. If you never contact them, you'll never know, but there's always a chance you won't love the dream client you've built up in your head, and if that's the case, remember you hold the power of choice.

Marketing and exploring new business relationships is a two-way street. You're assessing the suitability of the other party to become one of your clients just as much as you're aiming to show you're the perfect person to help them. If it turns out you've changed your mind once you have a clearer picture of how they work, well, now you know and can move on. That's business and everyone gets a choice.

Which also means that the other party might not believe you're their linguistic saviour.

How very dare they!

You may dread this response, but I'm sorry to say that your potential clients will sometimes say no. You will get rejected. People can 'reject' you *and* it doesn't mean you've screwed up. It can simply mean, for example, that they don't have a relevant project and rarely need translation. Your offer isn't aligned with what they want. Or they are perfectly happy with their current translation partner and existing set-up and see no compelling reason to change.

When this happens, you might veer between mortification and racking your brains to figure out what went wrong (probably nothing). You might opt for indignation "But they don't understand, their current translations are awful" or frustration "More fool them!" or berate yourself for not explaining the benefits clearly enough. Although all of the above reactions are natural, the correct response for an Explorer In Business is to view rejection as information and good feedback – see tracking your data in Chapter 6.

It's also an excellent opportunity to dig into the valuable reasons behind your rejection in case you uncover a hidden gem. Your future business partner might just need a few months before they need you and are saying "No, not right now", or they might have an excellent objection that you can ponder.

The journey to yes is paved with good objections

Some objections present a dead end: "We have no interest in translation, thank you very much". Others will take you only slightly off course: "our CEO does our translations because his wife is American". A tad awkward at first but with a bit of practice, easy enough to navigate. Objections are gold for your marketing because you can delve into why your marketing isn't landing and the surprise reasoning behind certain opinions. Often, these objections are common worries and concerns your potential clients have about working with you and so exploring ways to address them will strengthen your marketing. Add your freshly prepared, compelling responses to these objections to your marketing kit, and you'll be well equipped the next time they arise.

Even better, create a list of frequently asked questions on your website and/or sprinkle references to common concerns (and address them) throughout your marketing copy. Your future client will feel reassured that you understand their position and may be open to your perspective.

For instance, if you've been told you're too expensive so many times that you're seriously considering lowering your rates, hold on! Another perspective is that you're simply out of the company's expected budget and they aren't aware of the true costs of translation. Address this upfront by explaining how clients benefit from working with a professional like you and how investing in your reassuringly expensive service will deliver the outcome they want. Suddenly you're primed for a different conversation.

Get curious about each and every scenario and before you can say "Those damn dusky dolphins gave me an ear infection"[1], you'll be gathering the insights you need to handle a little turbulence.

Action

Take an objection you often hear in conversations about translation with potential clients or in response to a quotation.

---

1. Clearly not the dolphins' fault but yes, I did gain both an ear infection from my underwater antics and a prescription of high-dose antibiotics leaving me NZ$ 80 poorer. You win some, you lose some!

Can you find a solution?

Bonus points if you can present your counter-argument as a client-focused benefit.

Example

A common objection I've dealt with: We handle translations internally because one of our team members speaks fluent English.

A few responses I've used:

- Many of my clients also speak excellent English but they save so much time by working with me, which they can now spend on their core projects. (This led to one potential client admitting he didn't actually enjoy doing translations and would like to pass them on to someone else)

- It's always nice to have extra back-up or support during busy periods or holiday. There's so much content being produced nowadays and it can be hard to find people to help who understand your industry.

- Would it free up capacity if you had outside support or is that their full-time job? (Digging into how much they have to translate/produce in English)

* * *

Getting curious about the reasons behind these objections is part of being an Explorer in Business. Let's take a look at a couple of famous explorers to get some tips.

Chapter 8

Curious Explorers In Action

Curious people make for interesting people because they are always wondering – Why? What could happen? How? They are full of questions and hungry for the answers.

Explorers seek the answers to those questions by venturing outside their zone of expertise to find clues and tread the same path as those who know. So if you're going to follow in their footsteps, the only question to ask is: Are you going to take a gentle stroll or giant strides?

Natural progression or a fight for survival

Sir David Attenborough, broadcaster, biologist and natural historian, plays the long game and analyses the succession of tiny details that make a story. In short snippets of film (that no doubt take weeks, months or even years to capture) he zooms in on a single aspect of nature, using his storytelling talent to make the lifecycle of an unassuming plant as riveting as a fight between mountain gorillas. The natural curiosity he exudes draws you into the screen, keeping you on the edge of your seat to find out if the baby iguana survives or becomes prey to the killer snakes.

Bear Grylls is an adventurer who pits his survival skills against the harshest terrains. He bursts onto your screen with a faster pace of filming. His version of exploring is taking big risks, wading through piranha-infested mangrove swamps, battling with venomous creatures with the power to kill and working his way through the team's emergency first aid kit. His eye may be swollen shut but he emerges victorious, cooking that snake over an open fire – which, by the way, he started from a couple of rocks and wood.

As a translator, I suspect you take the Attenborough approach. Each sentence is examined under the microscope and the perfect phrase is teased out from the source language. It can take time to hunt down the answers, establish the facts, figure out what the author is really saying, consider the target audience, refine and polish your text.

When building your business you might believe you need to take a Grylls approach.[1] But there's a time and a place for

---

1. Off screen, he possesses a much calmer persona.

seat-of-your-pants survival adventures, and it's not in business. At least not the kind of business I want – with stress levels rising ever higher as you repeatedly refresh the screen, willing that overdue invoice to show as paid and on high alert for the next client project to win.

That high-stakes approach is not the way we should be thinking about marketing either. You shouldn't adopt an "all or nothing" strategy, chasing those rare five-figure contracts to the exclusion of all else. Opportunities can come in all shapes and sizes. You get the chance to spend a little time feeling your way and acclimatising to new scenarios. Build up to greater adventures in incremental steps.

Feed your curiosity

Take time to familiarise yourself with new surroundings and get to know the locals as part of each new experience – and I'll encourage you to focus on actual exploring and interaction rather than taking a wild guess and yet another training course. Your mission, should you choose to accept it, is to get closer to the heart of the action. Find out where your clients are and what they're talking about.

Gently does it though, pressing ahead little by little with quiet determination. If you move too swiftly, you'll miss those all-important details: The throwaway comment someone makes in the coffee break at an event that holds the answer to a manufacturer's translation sourcing process; or a "no thank you" received in response to a collaboration enquiry that presents the chance to ask for their actual requirements. Perhaps your first step is to team up with a more experienced colleague and ask for their insights so that you gain the confidence to test your assumptions in the field yourself.

Marketing is, in part, the process of getting curious about what might be possible, testing your messaging and exploring business opportunities. You ask a question, the other person tells you what they think or how they work. You can get curious and ask questions such as:
What's good and bad about their current set-up?
What would they love to happen in an ideal world if there were no restrictions?

If you're interested in the other person, you'll get far more useful information from an informal conversation than you ever would from attempting to impress your future clients with latest shiny shoddy tactics.

To make progress, you really do need those valuable insights and feedback from your target clients. Yet it can be difficult to put yourself in those uncomfortable and unfamiliar situations even if you know it's for the good of your profit margin. Besides taking incremental action, I have one more useful tip.

Take a swig from the bottle of adventurous spirit

What do you do in your everyday life that takes you slightly outside your comfort zone?

As humans, we don't like uncertainty. However, building up our tolerance over time will have an impact on all areas of our lives. There's nothing like travel to transport you to unfamiliar surroundings, but you probably can't do that as often as you'd like. Enter our everyday explorer adventures!

These can be as simple as joining a friend to try a new exercise class, taking a different route when out walking to see where you end up, or even trying a new food you're unsure about. By trying something new with an uncertain outcome, you're showing your brain that it's ok to trust new experiences and safe to not know what will happen. Even if you hate that new food, or the random trail that you took comes to a dead end, it's ok. Nothing horrendous happened and you now know the result. When incorporating this new-found adventurous spirit in your everyday life, you find yourself actively putting yourself in situations where the outcome is unknown, sure that whatever happens, you'l be fine. Then, when the time is right to stretch your comfort zone in business, you can draw on the experience you gained elsewhere to reduce any anxiety.

Looking back, I embarked on my first direct marketing campaign at roughly the same time as learning to unicycle. I put myself forward as a speaker at a chemistry trade show on my return from a business mastermind where we crafted hats and partied to Eurovision (amongst more strategic discussions). There just might be something in this 'new experience feeds brave new experience' malarkey.

Over time I've reframed marketing as a voyage of discovery and now adopt the mindset of an Explorer in Business. In all things work and life, sometimes you reach a dead end and have to backtrack a few steps to try again in a different direction. Occasionally, you reach your destination sooner than anticipated. More often than not, your route takes you to a new location via a few unexpected side excursions (not dastardly detours) as you discover more interesting opportunities off the beaten track.

> *"Exploration is curiosity put into action"*
> Don Walsh, oceanographer and explorer

Where will your curiosity take you first?

Action: What new experience will you try this week? Pick a new route, activity or area to explore. Push yourself a little outside the realms of your comfort zone and see what unfolds.

If you'd like me to cheer you on, let me know what you plan and how you felt afterwards! You can share your wins on social media and tag me in/use the hashtags: #TicketToExplore #ExplorersInBusiness

Chapter 9

Excited To Explore

You may have bought this book because you were frustrated with your current business set-up and the level of income you're bringing in. Marketing is a word that once had the power to terrify. It might even have led you to decide your existing clients were good enough, that they could be worse, and to convince yourself that all was fine after all. You might have avoided marketing because you were worried about doing the wrong thing, annoying your dream clients and blowing your chances of working with them forever.

I hope that now, at the end of this book, you can look at marketing through the eyes of a curious explorer, if not eager to pack your bags and set off on an adventure, then at least open and excited about the possibilities ahead. Take little steps, dip your toes in the water, take a gentle stroll through woodland, soaking up the scenery and seeing how the details in your surroundings all add up to a richer experience of life. The little details in the world your future clients inhabit will be easier to spot because you're looking at their world with curiousity and an eagerness to learn more. Your perspective will be different to theirs and that's a bonus – after all, as translators we're helping our clients translate their message into another language for another culture. We're all about different perspectives.

Adopting an explorer mindset means you'll finally start putting all those plans and projects you have into action (I know they're there, in a notebook or the darkest recesses of your mind). They might change, based on the insights you gain out in the wild, and that's ok.

I truly believe that exploring new ways to market yourself and having conversations with clients will raise the profile and importance of translators in the business world. Outreach to inspire the next generation of translators and interpreters at schools and universities is important, but we can have a greater impact on future translators and our own businesses if we are more visible right now.

Released from the quagmire

You might have found yourself stuck in analysis paralysis when confronted with the need to do marketing or felt that something undefined was holding you back. Whenever you feel that, try and dig a little deeper to figure out why. Chapter 3 offers one approach to avoid those dastardly detours that can take up so much of your precious time.

As much as I love a good adventure (I have voluntarily taken part in two mud obstacle runs, so I know how it feels to be literally stuck in the mud), feeling stuck in business is beyond frustrating. If I can get myself unstuck with a bit of guidance, you can too. Confidence comes from experience, and even then no one is truly an expert. Experimenting is key and obstacles in your path are to be expected, welcomed even, for the information they provide. And they're perfectly surmountable even if you have to take a little diversion.

Everyone's route and destination is unique and higher rates, direct clients and a successful business that you can be even prouder of are waiting just over the horizon.

Big leaps are optional, small steps still bring progress

Tackling marketing first as an undercover mission to "gather intelligence", shifted my mindset – and I want that for you. It's not always about taking huge leaps but instead, exploring and probing different options. That feels much easier and therefore we're more likely to do it. I don't have buckets of time, unwavering self-confidence or a villa that sleeps 20 with a designer swimming pool (who wants the cleaning and maintenance responsibilities?!) but I believe in myself more than before and find upleveling gradually a useful approach. I hope this approach helps you too. There are so many opportunities out there that you can either feel overwhelmed or excited by all the many possibilities! Adopt an explorer mindset and investigate what appeals.

'Professional contribution', or a nice side benefit of your exciting excursions

Being an Explorer in Business means meeting new people and so increasing your visibility. This is important not only to your business prospects, but also to our profession. Attend a client-facing event such as a trade fair or conference and you might be the first real-life translator the other attendees and speakers have met. You might be the only attending translator there.

The more translators there are out and about, virtually or in person, the greater the awareness of our industry and the value we can add. More people will discover the insights we can bring to a marketing campaign, research project or technical documentation aimed at an international audience. That's just a side benefit of your mini-marketing adventures, not a responsibility, but it's good to know your actions have a greater positive impact.

Action saves time

Be inspired and be curious by the great unknown, rather than apprehensive. Every step taken into your clients' world will help you build up a more detailed picture of the landscape and where you and your business might fit in. You'll also take action more quickly and be able to save time as you discover which terrains are less welcoming for your translation business travels.

Choose your adventure!

Please don't read this book, absorb the information, and then carry on as you were before. If you've identified beliefs or concerns that are still to be resolved, get curious about what's behind those thoughts, why you feel a certain way, and how you might shift your mindset or approach to make things easier. Take your newfound excitement about the prospect of marketing adventures and find a mini-adventure to gain that all-important experience and new insights into what your clients think, want and need. Take a micro-step that you can build on. And do get in touch with your questions, thoughts and feedback!

How far have you travelled?

At the start of this book I asked you to take a snapshot of where you were. Let's take a look at where you are now.

On a scale of one to ten, how you feel about marketing your business?

1 = I'll do everything I can to avoid it including, but not limited to, cleaning the toilet

10 = Lemme at it, I just need pointing in the right direction and I'm raring to go!

Thank you for letting me be your guide

Congratulations, you've earnt your ticket to explore! I hope you've enjoyed this jaunt into an alternative marketing mindset as much as I've enjoyed writing it and sharing my travel stories. If you're now bursting at the seams to start marketing your translation business and explore new business opportunities, then my job is done. It's time to start a new adventure!

The Explorer's Manifesto

- As an explorer, I will approach marketing with intrigue and curiosity

- I will take incremental steps to uplevel and acclimatise myself to new scenarios, stretching my comfort zone to seize new opportunities

- I will record my trail so that I have an incredible diary of my adventures and evidence to reveal whether I'm heading in the right direction

- I welcome motivation but will not rely on it, because I know that true progress is fuelled by me taking action

- I will keep my adventurous spirit topped up by regular mini adventures

- I know enough to go out and explore right now!

Adventures in marketing your translation business await!

References and Recommended Resources

Linnea Gandhi and Erik Johnson, *8 Things to Do Before You Run a Business Experiment*, Harvard Business Review, 2019 https://hbr.org/2019/02/8-things-to-do-before-you-run-a-business-experiment, accessed May 2023

James Clear, *Atomic Habits – An Easy and Proven Way to Build Good Habits and Break Bad Ones*, Random House, 2018

Books to bring out your adventurous spirit:

The Doorstep Mile by Alastair Humphreys

The Artist's Way by Julia Cameron

Explorers In Business

If you'd like to share your plans, I'd love to hear them. You can email me at Sarah@BusinessTranslated.com. And if you're not already receiving my free weekly email with marketing tips for translators, here's your VIP invitation to take a short trip over to **BusinessTranslated.com/TicketToExplore** to add that to your essential adventurer's kit. You'll also find photos to go with some of the stories mentioned in the book.

About the Author

Translator by day, explorer of new experiences and projects always.

I'm the type of person who volunteers to abseil down a block of flats, signs up for running challenges, enjoys mud obstacle runs, and unicycles badly. I love to travel but you'll also find me happy at home with a good book, experimenting in the kitchen or coming up with new marketing and business ideas.

Online, you can find me at ChemicalTranslator.com for German into English translation and editing services and BusinessTranslated.com for marketing motivation and training for translators.

Acknowledgements

Thank you, thank you, thank you

My editor and patient-ish husband Mark, also my current travel companion together with our sons. Julia Myring, my travel partner in crime – we farmed in Western Australia, kayaked in New Zealand, watched Kabuki in Tokyo, and cycled furiously away from ostriches in South Africa. Thank you Vicky Quinn Fraser, friend and book coach extraordinaire who introduced me and many others to the concept of a power-packed MicroBook (what you have right here in your hands). And a big thank you to my beta readers Mike Garner, Fiona Gray, Heike Holthaus, Alanah Reynor and Victoria Veldhoeven for all your feedback and making this final version so much better than the many drafts that came before.

www.ingramcontent.com/pod-product-compliance
Lightning Source LLC
Chambersburg PA
CBHW042129100526
44587CB00026B/4225